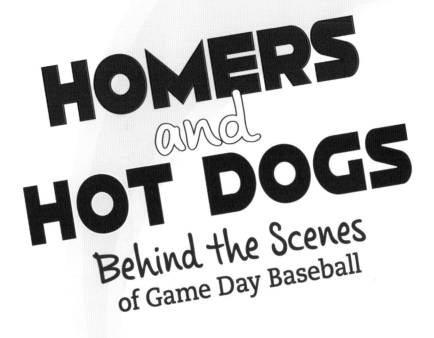

HOMERS and HOT DOGS

Behind the Scenes
of Game Day Baseball

by Martin Driscoll

CAPSTONE PRESS
a capstone imprint

Published by Spark, an imprint of Capstone.
1710 Roe Crest Drive, North Mankato, Minnesota 56003
capstonepub.com

Library of Congress Cataloging-in-Publication Data is available
on the Library of Congress website.

ISBN: 9781669003212 (hardcover)
ISBN: 9781669040330 (paperback)
ISBN: 9781669003175 (ebook PDF)

Summary: Think big-league baseball begins with the opening pitch? Think again! In this Sports Illustrated Kids book, go behind the scenes of a typical game day in Major League Baseball—from prepping the diamond and welcoming fans to hawking hot dogs and broadcasting from the booth. This fast-paced, fact-filled book will give baseball fans, young and old, a whole new perspective on America's favorite pastime.

Editor: Donald Lemke; Designer: Tracy Davies; Media Researcher: Svetlana Zhurkin; Production Specialist: Katy LaVigne

Image Credits
Associated Press: Danny Moloshok, 18, Janie McCauley, 19 (bottom), Julie Jacobson, 10, Kiichiro Sato, 11; Getty Images: Bart Young, 22, Brian Kersey, 23, Christian Petersen, 21, 25, 26, Duane Burleson, 14, Ed Zurga, 13, Elsa, 24, Jayne Kamin-Oncea, 8, 20, Jonathan Daniel, 15, Jupiterimages, 28, Rich Schultz, 9, Rob Carr, 17; Newscom: Fort Worth Star-Telegram/Rodger Mallison, 27; Shutterstock: Arina P. Habich, 29 (top), Bada1, 16 (bottom middle), Dan Thornberg, cover (top right), 1, Eugene Onischenko, cover (top), Frank Romeo, 12, James Kirkikis, 6, Keith J. Finks, 16 (top), Kelsey Fox, 16 (bottom right), M. Budniak, 29 (bottom), Philip Eppard, cover (bottom middle), planet5D LLC, 19 (top), Ron Dale (background), cover, back cover, Stephen Reeves, cover (bottom right), Tiny Bubble, 16 (bottom left), zoff, cover (bottom left); Sports Illustrated: Al Tielemans, 7, Erick W. Rasco, 4, 5

Printed and bound in the USA. 5195

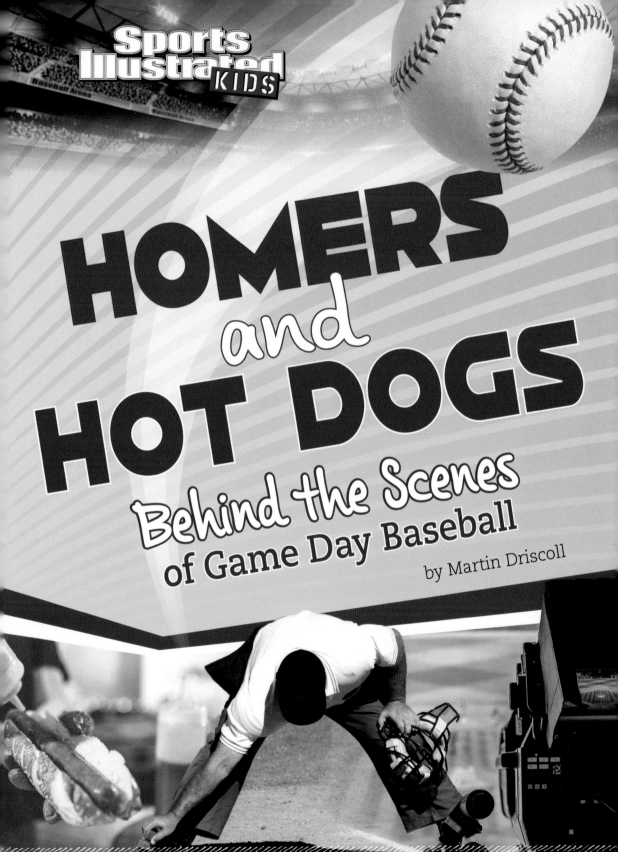

Sports Illustrated KIDS

HOMERS
and
HOT DOGS
Behind the Scenes
of Game Day Baseball

by Martin Driscoll

TABLE OF CONTENTS

Words in **bold** are in the glossary.

THE CRACK OF THE BAT

A Major League Baseball (MLB) game is about to begin. The pitcher throws a fastball. The batter swings. *Crack!* He hits a flyball to an outfielder. The batter is out, and the home fans roar.

Even the sounds of a ballgame are exciting. But game day begins long before the first pitch!

Washington Nationals fans during the 2019 World Series

STARTING EARLY

Game day starts early for the grounds crew. They cut the grass and paint the foul lines. They rake the infield dirt. They pack the dirt into place around home plate and the pitcher's mound.

Phillies grounds crew at Citizens Bank Park in Philadelphia, Pennsylvania

A coach rolls a cart onto the infield grass. It holds 200 baseballs. Time for batting practice!

A coach has the job of pitching for batting practice. Most players get to hit. They stretch or play catch when it's not their turn. They may also **shag** balls in the outfield.

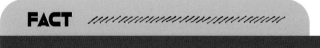

New York Yankees players at batting practice

The clubhouse is a home away from home. Players get ready for action. The team provides food before every game. Players can grab all the bubble gum they want.

Outfielder Michael Conforto in the New York Mets clubhouse

The Chicago Cubs clubhouse

A clean game uniform hangs in every player's locker. The equipment manager makes sure players have everything they need.

The starting pitcher heads onto the field about 45 minutes before game time. First he stretches. Then he gets onto a pitching mound. He throws soft pitches at first. Then he throws pitches at full speed.

Former Houston Astros pitcher Gerrit Cole

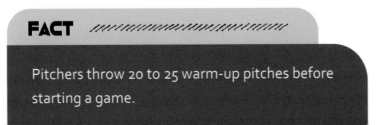

FACT //

Pitchers throw 20 to 25 warm-up pitches before starting a game.

The home plate umpire is in charge.

He checks the baseballs before each game.

Each ball has been rubbed with a special mud.

Balls can't be too shiny or slick.

The head umpire also takes the **lineups** from the managers. He sweeps the dirt off home plate when it is time to "Play ball!"

The stands are packed with fans. The fans are ready to cheer. They are also ready to eat. Hot dogs, peanuts, and nachos are fan favorites.

Vendors walk the stadium aisles with a lot of different foods.

Workers make food at Nationals Park in Washington, D.C.

Workers at the **concession** stands keep busy making and selling all that food. They often sell 10,000 or more hot dogs during a game.

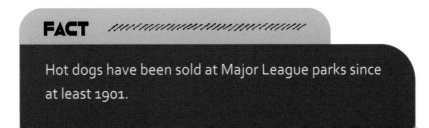

FACT

Hot dogs have been sold at Major League parks since at least 1901.

ACTION PACKED

People in the press box watch the game closely. **Broadcasters** describe the action for TV and radio. They share news about the players and teams.

Reporters also work in the press box.
They write about the game for newspapers
and websites.

Each team has a **dugout** beside the field. Players rest on the bench when they are not on the field. They wait for their turn at bat.

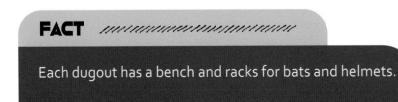

FACT

Each dugout has a bench and racks for bats and helmets.

Their manager also watches from the dugout. He is in charge. As the game goes on, he might decide to change pitchers.

Chicago Cubs manager David Ross

STRETCH TIME

Players get tired as the game goes on. Fans do, too. They get a break in the middle of the seventh inning. Fans stand and sing "Take Me Out to the Ball Game." They stretch their legs. That's why it's called the seventh-inning stretch.

Colorado Rockies mascot Dinger entertaining fans

Fans singing during the seventh-inning stretch at the Wrigley Field in Chicago, Illinois

FACT ///////////////////////////////////////

The grounds crew keeps working during games. They rake the infield dirt after the third and sixth innings.

Bullpen at Minute Maid Park in Houston, Texas

The game has reached the late innings. The manager makes a call to the **bullpen**. That's where relief pitchers await a chance to get into the game. The manager tells one of them to get ready.

When the bullpen door swings open, he jogs toward the infield. The home fans cheer for their **closer**.

Former LA Dodgers relief pitcher Kenley Jansen

The third-base coach has been busy all game. When his team is batting, he sends signals to hitters and baserunners. He might pull on his ear to tell a runner to steal a base.

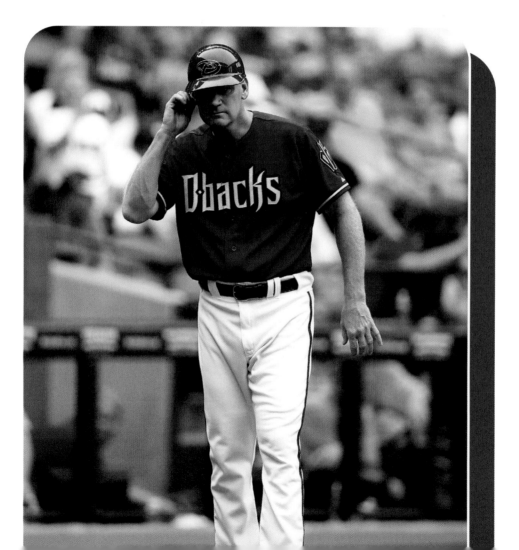

Texas Rangers third-base coach signals Elvis Andrus to head home.

The score is tied in the ninth inning. The home team has a runner on second. When the batter gets a hit, the third-base coach waves his arm. He wants the runner to head for home. The runner is safe, and the home team wins!

FACT

The grounds crew is still working after the game. They repair the area around home plate and on the pitcher's mound.

PLAN YOUR GAME DAY

You can host game day at your house!

- Make your own tickets to invite friends over and watch a game.

- Ask everyone to wear your team's colors.

- Have popcorn or peanuts ready to go.

- Bring on the hot dogs! Add relish, onions, cheese, and other toppings you like. Don't forget ketchup and mustard.

GLOSSARY

broadcaster (BRAHD-kast-uhr)—a person who describes the game on television or radio

bullpen (BUHL-pehn)—the area where relief pitchers warm up; usually found behind the outfield wall

closer (KLOH-zuhr)—a relief pitcher who is brought in to get the final outs of the game

concession (kuhn-SEH-shuhn)—a place where food and drinks are sold in the ballpark

dugout (DUHG-owt)—one of the shelters where players and coaches sit during games

lineup (LYE-nuhp)—a list of the starting players and the batting order

shag (SHAG)—to catch flyballs and field groundballs in the outfield during batting practice

READ MORE

Berglund, Bruce. *Big-Time Baseball Records*. North Mankato, MN: Capstone, 2022.

Nelson, Robin. *The Story of a Baseball Bat: It Starts with Wood.* Minneapolis: Lerner Books, 2021.

Omoth, Tyler. *Baseball Fun*. North Mankato, MN: Capstone, 2021.

INTERNET SITES

Baseball Training World: 15 Fun Baseball Facts for Kids
baseballtrainingworld.com/15-fun-baseball-facts-for-kids/

Kiddle: Baseball Facts for Kids
kids.kiddle.co/Baseball

MLB Kids
mlb.com/fans/kids

INDEX

ABOUT THE AUTHOR

Martin Driscoll is a former newspaper reporter and longtime editor of children's books. He is also the author of several sports books for children, including biographies of legendary stars of boxing, baseball, and basketball. Driscoll lives in southern Minnesota with his wife and two children.